OUR GREED & IGNORANCE:
Poses A Far Greater Threat To America, Than
Terrorism

By

Jim Green

Dedicated To:

All who seek the truth….

Where is the truth in America? If America fails it will have two parents: GREED AND IGNORANCE—Greed on the part of the 1%, and Ignorance by those in the 99% who are in the "bubble", and who are unwilling, or unable to inform themselves, and thus vote Republican—a truth in America, today—and Republican Conservative, and 30-year Congressional insider, Mike Lofgren, nailed it regarding the Republican Party, today--with the "Republicans went crazy"….

ISBN-13: 978-1479246335

ISBN-10: 1479246336

PROLOGUE

Paul Ryan is not a decent person. Why does our media not tell the truth regarding this person—the unvarnished truth? Like his mendacity at the Republican Convention—telling one lie after another--and how can he claim to be a champion of deficit reduction—and rail against President Obama—when he voted to add $7 trillion to our deficit under Bush!

What a hypocrite! And the "Nuns On A Bus" nailed him for his anti-Christian views—Ryan claims to be a "Christian"—if one is not following he teachings of Christ—they are NOT a Christian— [and this net can be drawn over the entire Republican agenda]-- so why does our media not confront them on their views?

Ryan is only one of many in the current Republican line-up, however—And, where is the Republican apology? Apparently aware of the problem, and that the question would be asked, Romney jumped out ahead with his book "No Apology"—

When, in fact, neither Romney nor any Republican for national office should be permitted to say even one word in this election—until they first profusely apologize to the American people for the damage Republicans have done to America, when they have been in the White House, over the past 32 years!

It is the decent thing to do! A decent person would have done this long ago—during the Republican debates! And, where was our media calling for this apology during the debates? It is our only assurance that the Republicans will never again put America in peril, if elected!

For instance, our deficit was $60 billion in 1980—
and like a juvenile delinquent with their parent's
stolen credit card—the Republicans ran up debt
on the American people to a staggering criminal
$10 trillion by 2008—and it has cost an additional
$5 trillion, mostly in corporate welfare, to bring
this runaway train under control—with some
economists calling for even more to correct the
damage done as a result of the Republicans being
in the White House!

"Stupid" is crass, street language—to be used
sparingly—and used because it is the best word in
the interest of getting at the Truth---also, the
reference, here, is not regarding individual IQ, but
rather, for instance, their claim to be the pro-
market "free enterprise" party—when more
businesses have failed as a direct result of
Republican policies than at any other time in
American history!

The agenda of the Republican Party, today, is "Greed For The Sake Of Greed" --Period, they have no other agenda—[no investment in the betterment of America]—and the sole objective of the Republicans in Congress is to pander to this GREED—it is "stupid" because it is anti-capitalism—this posture is anti-the business community—and our business failures are the proof! The Republican agenda, today, is solely to make the already rich, richer--

Ryan and company want to do away with Social Security and Medicare—because it doesn't "pander to the greed of the Republican's wealthiest contributors" [to eliminate their paying taxes]—and Romney wants to cut their taxes even further!

There is a bright line between cut taxes for the 1%, and eliminate America's social safety net—and it is driven solely by GREED!

Ryan, et al are stupid because of their indifference to a weapon available to President Obama, not available to FDR—specifically, if it were not for our Social Security and military retirement moneys percolating up through our economy—we would not be talking about having narrowly averted another Great Depression—we would be buried in one!

Social Security—our social insurance--is a Pro-Market solution!

In short, it is stupid for the Republicans to undermine these social programs—because even our most greedy will be injured in the long run!

We can't siphon America's wealth away from the consuming middle [and particularly for the shallow objective of greed, just for the sake of greed]—without sending our economy into meltdown!

Reaganomics has a shelf-life of about 7 years before the economy collapses—as we learned in 1987 [when the stock market lost a quarter of its value in one day], and again 2008—and the American taxpayers had to rush in, in both cases, with trillions of dollars to prevent the imminent collapse of our economy!

Another annoying element in the Republican propaganda blather, today, is the nonsense that Reagan was a "great" president—Reagan wasn't even mediocre—relegating America to the 8th Century when we had kings and serfs--isn't "revolutionary"—it is a rejection of modernity—and history will record that Reagan was the worst president in American history, until Bush II bumped him out of last place!

So why is our media allowing the Republicans to get away with this BS?

The national Republicans Party, today, has traded GOP for NDP [Not Decent People]—Rove, Limbaugh, Ryan, Glenn Beck [the list is almost endless] in this strata—and it is time we started fessing up to the truth in America!

In sum, the agenda of the national Republican Party, today, is based on the exact same tactic as Hitler's "Big Lie"—and it is equally as deceptive and despicable—no decent person would advocate what Romney and Ryan are advocating!

And it is directed at our ignorant and those suffering from feelings of low self-esteem—those who are awash in magical and wishful thinking, theological terrorism, and those who are suffering from amnesia [What R & R are advocating has a track record—IT DOESN'T WORK]! And their pitch is to cover up their real agenda: To make our already rich, richer—Period, the national Republican Party stands for NOTHING else!

The following letters expand on the above—and as Oscar Wilde averred "The only truly worthless opinion is an unbiased one"—so bias, agreed—but always in the interest in getting at the larger goal—the truth....

Finally, a note to the reader—the letters are mostly letters to the editor, relative at the time--not in sequence, and some redundancy [please look for the nuggets....]—also, if you are a "typo-wonk"— are more concerned with sentence structure, etc., than content—you probably won't like my writing—and a wayward capital letter, here and there, and appearing out of place and used for emphasis—editorial license—so apologies, here—

Just look for content, please....THX

CHAPTER ONE

The More We Change, The More We Stay The Same....

Editor/NY Times:

A Republican candidate for president said "On next January 20, there will begin in Washington, the biggest unraveling, unsnarling, untangling operation in our nation's history."

But before Republican ideologues say "right on" regarding President Obama—this was from an archive speech by Republican candidate Tom Dewey, and directed at President Truman, in 1948.

Will politics never change? Given the political rhetoric you would think President Truman couldn't even tie his own shoes—albeit, he had ended WWII [while President Obama has rescued America from another Great Depression].

And other parallels between these two elections are even more striking.

For instance, Truman was outraged by what he called a "Do nothing Congress"—and he went on the warn the electorate that "The country cannot afford another Republican Congress." Are we in an echo chamber, here?

The most startling parallel, however, is when Truman said of the Republican Congress on a stump speech "It is a sad tale of the sell out of the American people to these gluttons of privilege—these cold men who skim the cream from our natural resources to satisfy their own greed."

This could have been said yesterday, and yet, it was said by President Truman 64 years ago!

Finally, President Truman offered some words of wisdom to the American electorate on the danger or returning our government back to the Republicans [as true today, as then] "I'm just waking you up to the fact that this is YOUR fight—and YOU are going to be the loser [if you return the White House back to the Republicans]."

And, as every student of History knows, and in spite of the inexcusable headline error by the Chicago Tribune "DEWEY DEFEATS TRUMAN"— President Truman won.

Jim Green, Democrat candidate for Congress, 2000

CHAPTER TWO

The Truth About Healthcare:

Editor/NY Times:

It is amazing the people, mostly Tea Party, railing against the Patient Protection and Affordable Care Act (PPACA), signed into law by President Obama, on March 23, 2010.

The truth is, the only persons in the rank and file who are railing against PPACA, are those who don't know what we have now…

Don't they know they have been duped? Made suckers of by the "profit-takers" [who don't even so much as put a Band-Aid on a patient]--who skim tens of billion of dollars out of our healthcare system in America—purely in the name of GREED!

Our healthcare system in America is an $800 billion a year industry [17% of our GDP], and the "profit-takers" claim an obscene 30% [almost a third] in "administrative costs"—when those costs are only 5–7% in every other major country in the world! Do the math—It is unlawful to make a "profit" from people's healthcare, in every country except America!

And tens of millions of the "profit" they take out of our healthcare system is used for propaganda ads to make suckers out of the Tea Party, etc—

Ever notice how they throw around the word "Freedom"—they are not talking about OUR freedom—us, the American people—they are talking about THEIR freedom to go on making a pot of gold off of the American people!

And it makes you wonder how many of those protesting in DC, many paid by the "profit-takers" to be there—are not protesting the requirement that everyone who drives must have liability insurance? It is the same principle—and it also drives down the cost---After all, this is a Republican law in Massachusetts—that is, before it became "socialism"-----

The truth is, we pay twice as much for healthcare in America as every other major industrial country—and yet, we are 37th in the world in quality of care, according the World Health Organization—we have the highest infant mortality rate in the world, and overall mortality ranked along side some Third World countries—

And solely because we have a few siphoning billions out of our "for profit" healthcare system—for their personal GREED [hint, not one dime goes to the healthcare of anyone]!

It should be no surprise, then, that they have spent tens of millions in propaganda ads to trick the Tea Party, and other uninformed Americans about

PPACA. [What a double-cross, using OUR money to rip us off]!

And, also it should be no surprise that the Republican candidates for president support this rip-off of the American people—because they don't represent us, folks—their ONE AND ONLY program is to pander to the GREED of their wealthiest contributors—PERIOD! They have no other program!

Finally, a few myths need to be exploded—There is NO 'free" healthcare—England, or elsewhere-- never has been, never will be—Also, insurance, is insurance—whether car, house or health—WE take it out, and pool our money to share the costs—for OUR protection, if fate taps us on the shoulder—

And yet, at present, 44,000 Americans die every year, solely, because of the excessive costs of health insurance [and so the "profit-takers" can get their piece of the action]—And the biggest myth—no one responsible is saying that medical professionals should not be compensated for their years of training—a GP in England earns on average $200,000—but no one wants a system, including doctors, where persons enter the medical field as a means to get rich, rather than treat the ill.

Jim Green, Democrat candidate for Congress, 2000 www.Inclusivism.org

CHAPTER THREE

THE HISTORY OF HOW WE GOT WHERE WE ARE:

In the mid-1970's, the colliding forces of automation, technology, globalization, etc., reached a critical mass, resulting in ubiquitous unemployment in all of the OECD countries, and has left their leaders conflicted, ever since, regarding the displaced employee—Eurozone unemployment is still in double digits, with Spain at 22.9%, and with high youth unemployment a major factor in Arab Spring.

In the U.S., we took a pro-active role in addressing, and as a direct response to this economic shift—and in 1978 President Carter signed into law 15 USC § 3101--which "authorizes" the creation of a "reservoir of public employment" at any time our unemployment in America exceeds "3%".

The following year, in 1979, however, and in a panic over Humphrey-Hawkins—our ultra-conservative foundations, and desperate to preserve the "market only" job creation concept, embraced a flawed paper by an obscure MIT student, David L. Birch "The Job Generation Process"; and [with lots of cash] gave his paper biblical importance, and every president since has cited his finding as gospel.

Birch's paper concluded that "small businesses" were the greatest generator of new jobs—problem is, for the purposes of policy-making—it is BS. In a study at Harvard University in 2010, "The Myth of Small Business Job Creation" The research shows "no systematic relationship between firm size and growth." And that small businesses can actually detract from job growth—nevertheless, it is still the Republican One and Only job creation solution!

And in spite of this Washington struggles, still, to make this antiquated and unworkable notion, work--that it is only the market that can create jobs—the world has changed, our solutions haven't, and the result has been a disaster, politically as well as otherwise!

It would be impossible to still have 8.3% unemployment if we were on the right path [the result is the proof]—and among other problems with this concept--if the market fails, the unemployed are out of luck [It is the reason Romeny's job creation solution is a farce!].

Further, unemployment is a "social" problem we are seeking to address with a highly unstable, incompatible entity: The Market --That is, the last place we should look for a reliable solution to our unemployment crisis is The Market....

And, what apparently isn't clear going forward in the 21st Century, is that an expanding and contracting public workforce is an INDISPENSABLE component to the correct functioning of a modern market economy—i.e., The Humphrey-Hawkins Full Employment Act was dead-on correct in 1978—and provided a "win-win" solution for America--

The market thrives when we have a robust, employed, consuming workforce, and it is essential to consumer confidence—and overlooked is that HR 870 [currently in Committee], and the proposed "Neighbor-To-Neighbor Job Creation Act" [hereafter NTN] See: www.Inclusivism.org [both authorized under Humphrey-Hawkins], are deficit-neutral--Pro-Market "win-win" solutions: The American people win, and capitalism wins—

CHAPTER FOUR

Editor/NY Times

There will be a lot of "buyer's remorse" on the part of rank and file Republicans—who voted for Romney/Ryan—if they should actually win—

They will be like the guy who woke up from a serious hangover and found out he had thrown the family cat through the neighbor's window [an old Shelley Berman joke]—

Most of the rank and file I have talked to are so blindly zealous in their vote "against" President Obama—[some based on racism]--they don't have a clue what Romney/Ryan has in store for them.

Specifically, to pick up right where Bush II left off—and we all know how that turned out! Been there—did that—it is called "Supply-Side" or

"Reaganomics"—IT DOESN'T WORK! IT IS WHAT CAUSED THE GREAT RECESSION IN 2008!

The national Republican Party has but a single agenda—TO PANDER TO THE GREED OF THEIR WEALTHIEST CONTRIBUTORS! Period! That's it—and rather than investing in the betterment of America, they hide their wealth in secret bank accounts to avoid investing in America--!

Further, we can't siphon America's wealth away from the consuming middle, and give it to the already wealthy, without sending our economy into a tailspin!

"Supply-Side" has a shelf-life of about 7 years before the false premise upon which it is based starts caving in on itself—as we learned in our economic collapse in 1987 and again in 2008 [and getting worse each salvo from this corrupt scheme]—and it has cost the American taxpayers trillions of dollars to put a floor under our economy, in the inevitable meltdown!

President Obama had the grim task, from his first day in office, of saving America from another Great Depression, in 2009—

And the Republican propaganda machine has the gall to snow the rank and file with the false blather [flat out lie] that Obama was a "tax and spend" liberal—Obama is a moderate CONSERVATIVE! And if McCain had been elected he would have taken the exact same steps—the choice was "Stimulus" or an ultra-severe Depression—Period! We were losing 700,000 jobs a month!

Finally, the starting point in our political discussion in this election—MUST begin with a Republican apology as assurance to the American people they will not return to the same failed policies that almost sunk America!

So what rank and file Republicans should be asking, now, is where is the Romney/Ryan profuse apology to the American people for the damage Republican policies have done to America?

Jim Green, Democrat candidate for Congress, 2000 See also: My Letters To President Obama, on Amazon/Kindle

CHAPTER FIVE

Editor/NY Times [re Republican debates]:

Has anyone noticed that the Republican candidates for president are selling themselves—NOT on the basis of real solutions, but rather because they are the candidate who can "beat Obama"—

It is a goal that is consummate proof that "winning" trumps what is in the best economic interest of the voter—and no one would vote against their own pocketbook, would they?

Indeed, talk about bad ideas regarding their "solutions"—every Republican candidate wants to return America to the same policies that drove our economy into a ditch in the first place!

To wit, Cut taxes for the 1%, they will build factories with the extra cash—everyone will have a job in the corporation—and we will all live happily ever after—

Yes folks, it's a fairy tale!

In fact, with the extra cash the 1% bought an extra yacht, or more trips to Europe—and by siphoning America's wealth out of the hands of the consuming middle, and into their hands—our economy went into meltdown—TWICE—in 1987 & 2008—

So where was the Tea Party regarding the "stimulus" spending in 1987? Where was their hue and cry that Reagan was a "tax and spend liberal" when he used the exact same economic tool to put a floor under our collapsing economy in 1987?

Indeed, Supply-Side has a shelf-life of about 7 years before the economy goes into meltdown—and it has taken trillions of dollars added to our deficit—IN BOTH OF THESE YEARS—to clean up the mess!

Supply-Side is the major reason America has a $15 trillion deficit—our deficit was only $60 billion in 1980—the government cannot cut off its revenue so it can give a big fat paycheck to the 1%--and add the shortfall in revenue to our deficit for our grandchildren to pay—WITHOUT DRIVING AMERICA INTO MASSIVE DEBT!

Return to this—where is the Republican apology?

Folks, the Goldwater era Republican doesn't exist anymore—for one, he was pro-choice and approved of gays in the military—and America wasn't distracted from our real issues, by these wedge issues—and added into the mix by Republicans, today, so the voter will be looking away from what they are REALLY UP TO:

Specifically, the national Republican Party, today, has only ONE program—to pander to the GREED of their wealthiest contributors—PERIOD, That's it—they have NO other program!

In short, folks, turning America over to the current Republican agenda is analogous to handing the keys to our new Cadillac to a fallen-down drunk—who wrecked our car last week—would anyone in touch with reality do this? Don't answer that….

Jim Green, www.Inclusivism.org

CHAPTER SIX

Letter to the editor:

THIS IS A TEST: The following are two political speeches—the question is, were they made by a Republican or a Democrat? Were they made by the same candidate, and if not, what candidate most likely made the respective speeches—and how relevant are the respective speeches to the problems we face today? Don't peek—the answer is at the bottom—

Speech One:

"Folks, we live in an era of great challenge-- our people are a hearty, industrial people—and they can meet that challenge....Industry means employment and that employment means a fair wage for anybody who wants to work—and I mean to see that we get there....".

Speech Two:

"Ladies and Gentlemen, we have met today at a cross-roads—these are not ordinary times—we meet at a cross-roads in history. For far too long the wrong roads have been taken—the wrong roads have led us into war, into poverty, into unemployment and inflation. May I say to you, we have reached the turning-point—No longer will 'We the people' suffer for the benefit of the few.

Now I would lie to you if I told you the roads would be easy—they will not be easy—nothing that is right and good has ever been easy. 'We the people' know that—and we know the right roads and the good. Today, I say to you—We are the people, you and I—and it is time to let the people rule. Thank You"

Speech Two was written for, and given by Charles Palentine, a fictions candidate for president in the noted movie "Taxi Driver", a film made in 1976 [36 years ago].

Speech One was made by John M. Staton [a real person and a real speech]—the Governor of Georgia—the speech was made in 1911 [over 100 years ago—Staton was a Democrat]—

What is that maxim—"The more things change, the more they stay the same".

Jim Green, Democrat candidate for Congress, 2000

CHAPTER SEVEN

Editor/NYTimes:

Gore Vidal refers to America as the "United States of Amnesia"—his reference is to how quickly we seem to forget atrocious government policy--

And the Republican candidates are trying to capitalize on this by blurring the line regarding our current economic recovery—

Even appealing to those with a short-term memory loss by hinting that President Obama may have caused our economic meltdown—even though he had not even been elected president at that time—

And in their desperation to regain the White House they would not have anything good to say about President Obama if he had saved them from drowning—

Serious discussion about real issues—essential to an informed electorate--gets lost in the minutia—it is little wonder it has been dubbed the "Silly Season"—

The truth is—"Supply-Side Economics" resulted in atrocious government policies—that run up massive deficits for our grandchildren to pay--drove our economy into a ditch—and all of the Republican candidates—save for Ron Paul—have told us they will return to this failed economic model—if elected!

The truth is, our deficit was only $60 billion in 1980—and in every year since, when Republicans held the White House—they have added to our deficit, driving it up to a staggering $10 trillion by the time Bush II left office!

The interest, alone, on this debt is $400 billion annually—almost 2/3rds of our Defense Budget!

Further it is pure bull that Republicans and Democrats share equally in the disaster caused by Supply-Side—the Democrats had control of Congress only one year during Reagan's two terms—the last year—and only the last two years of Bush II, but by then most of the damage had already been done—and at NO time did they have sufficient votes to override a presidential veto—

Further, calling for Republicans to apologize is two-fold: Absent an apology the Republicans in Congress are arrogant—like they have pulled off the Brink's robbery and gotten away with it—and compounded by a press too timid [to be kind] to demand they be held accountable—and secondly, they have not said anything, up to now, to affirm that they will not pick up where Bush II left off, if elected! In fact, their "no tax increase on the wealthy" is consummate proof of it--

For the Republicans in the House it is "Don't confuse me with facts"—

President Obama was forced to use deficits to clean up the mess caused by the reckless Republicans policies of the past 8 years—it was the only medicine available—according to every credible economist in American, on the right or left! And McCain would have been forced to take the exact same action—if he wanted to prevent America from going into another Great Depression!

So the "blank check" lie put out by Boehner—suggesting that President Obama is a "tax and spend" liberal—is a contemptible lie!

Further, How on earth can anyone or any political party hold themselves up to the champions in cutting the deficit—WHEN THEIR PARTY CAUSED IT!

Jim Green

CHAPTER EIGHT

President Obama/Fellow Democrats:

For the past 65 years we have had two parallel paths to address unemployment in America—

To assure employment for the troops returning from WW II, President Truman signed into law The Full Employment Act of 1946—

This was expanded upon in 1978 with the Humphrey-Hawkins Full Employment Act, signed into law by President Carter—

And a 21st Century version of this path to full employment in America, is pending the House, HR 870.

Humphrey-Hawkins best defines this path to addressing unemployment in America, and it authorizes our government to create a "reservoir of public employees" anytime our unemployment rises above "3%".

And in spite of the fact that this path to employment has been the law of the land since 1946—and is a Pro-Market solution [more on this shortly]---Washington has lacked the wherewithal to implement this path to employment on behalf of the American people—[a point not lost on the "occupy" movement].

Rather, Washington has taken the alternate parallel path—by insisting that human labor is a "component" in the free enterprise system—[barely distinguishable from the machine the human operates] to be used and discarded "at will"—and that it is an attack upon "freedom" to challenge this concept, but whose "freedom"?

As a result, however, "conventional wisdom" has insisted that it is the market, alone, that can fix our unemployment crisis—the result has been a disaster—

The market thrives when we have a robust, employed, consuming public—and by taking this parallel path—we not only have a staggering 9% unemployment, but a struggling recovery as well.

Ironically, following WW II, Australia passed a law very similar to our Full Employment Act of 1946—

Difference is—they actually put it into effect—and over the next 30 years—[until the cold winds of conservatism swept in Reagan and Thatcher, etc.] –the government in Australia saw as a solemn responsibility that "anyone willing to work should be provided with a job" [a quote from the "Audacity of Hope"].

The citizens of Australia still refer to this 30 years as their "Golden Age".

Jim Green, Democrat candidate for Congress, 2000 www.Inclusivism.org

CHAPTER NINE

Editor/NY Times:

FDR urged us to put ending unemployment on a war footing—and it is the failure of the OECD countries to follow the wisdom in this observation, particularly in Greece, Spain and the U.S.—that has their economies in trouble today—

A large part of the problem is that we are victims of our own success—while we have grown more and more efficient in the marketplace, we have become less efficient with what to do with the fallout—we celebrate innovation and then are befuddled with what to do with the 9 persons who are displaced in the workplace by the innovation—

And in the mid–1970's the colliding mega-forces—automation, globalization, innovation, technology, etc., reached a critical mass resulting in ubiquitous unemployment in all of the OECD countries—

In the U.S. the result was a "malaise"—as we turned to the market to fix itself—a mind-set that continues to this day—

Over the past 65 years our Congress, and two American presidents [Truman & Carter], have stepped up to the plate and passed laws to end unemployment in America—but inexplicably these laws have never been enforced—

Specifically, the Humphrey-Hawkins Full Employment Act [15 USC § 3101] authorizes the government/president to create a "reservoir of public employees"—at any point in which our unemployment in America rises above "3%" [and we are three times over the percent necessary, at present, to trigger this law]—

But in spite of the fact that it is a Pro-Market solution—[the market thrives when we have a robust, employed, consuming public]—and we can fund without adding a dime to our deficit—an antiquated mind-set has prevented enforcement of these laws—

In short, the world has changed, our solutions haven't, and the result has been a disaster! We are Hell-bent on fixing our unemployment crisis with "private sector jobs"—[a concept antithetical to capitalism]—and the result has been a disaster—

Accordingly, the minute our Debt Ceiling crisis is behind us [the Republicans grow up!]—Congress is urged to pass the Neighbor-To-Neighbor Job Creation Act: A federally mandated, mutual insurance, owned by our employed to provide the funds to hire/train our unemployed, See:

www.Inclusivism.org and HR 870 [currently in Committee].

The truism is that fixing unemployment is an indispensable component in fixing an economy—and the proposed, here, is a Pro-Market "win-win" solution—the American people win, and capitalism wins!

Jim Green, Democrat candidate for Congress, 2000

CHAPTER TEN

THE FAIL-SAFE ELECTRONIC VOTING ACT:

So long as the potential for manipulation of electronic voting continues to exist—our elections in America will be in peril! In spite of all the polls showing a strong Obama victory--it was not until 10PM Central on 11-4-08.....that we could breath a sigh of relief....we had been cheated out of the past two elections....with many believing that Bush was never legally elected president of the United States....and we were braced for the worst.......this can, and MUST be fixed before 2010, so that this never happens again, and in the interest of all who support fair and open elections--regardless of party. Accordingly, it is urged that we adopt the following proposed "FAIL-SAFE ELECTRONIC VOTING ACT":

THE FAIL-SAFE ELECTRONIC VOTING ACT

1) EVERY electronic voting machine (hereafter EVM), must be inexpensive, identical throughout the U.S. in a 1/150 ratio, and *must count and produce a hard-copy of the recorded votes*. In addition, an extra copy of their recorded votes would be produced (not necessarily a hard-copy), marked "Voter's Copy", and containing "NOTICE: Do Not Destroy Until Every Election On Your Ballot Is Certified". [If Wal-Mart handed us a piece of paper with the words "trust us" as a receipt for our purchases—we would be outraged—and this is our current electronic voting nightmare—but in this case it is our democracy at risk]!

2) *After confirming that their votes are recorded correctly,* the voter would then insert the hard-copy ballot into a software-free (count only) optical scanner (hereafter OS), for a second count. The hard-copy ballot would be retained by election officials in the event a candidate asks for a recount (*not possible under the current system, and which undermines the legality of each such*

election). The EVM and the OS must be manufactured by different companies (which is universally true today).

3) Election officials assigned to oversee the EVM, would be prevented by law from overseeing the OS, and vice-versa, and stiff criminal penalties would be imposed for violations.

4) Further, every EVM would be programmed with raw data re the total registration rolls, by party, and norms for their voting history, etc.,----as an "alert" to a possible irregularity, such as an "Under-vote"—or "vote-flipping" etc., and *standards* established to suspend certification where there is an "improbable result", at least temporarily, of a particular election until the discrepancy is cleared up. (This is what computers do best, and it would be very easy to create such a program).

5) At the end of the election day, tallies would be

taken from the EVM and the OS, for each candidate. *If the tallies didn't balance for any given election, or if there is an "alert", that election cannot be certified until the "error" is corrected.* If the candidates agree (the victory is certain), minor discrepancies in the count could be disregarded. While probably rare, the Voter, or a random sample of Voters, would be required by law to return their Copy of the recorded votes to the election office to clear up any "error", or where an "alert" signals the need for same.

6) Further, every state provides for a recount when the total vote falls below a certain percent of difference between the candidates, impossible to conduct with the current EVM—and thus Congress must mandate the following regarding presidential candidates: A RUN-OFF election is mandated and triggered in those states where the percent of total vote is less than .5% of difference between any given candidates; said election to be held on the second Saturday following the

election, on PAPER BALLOTS ONLY, and contain ONLY the names of the relevant candidates, for instance: "Barack Obama, Democrat" and "John McCain, Republican"—with oversight in counting by a representative(s) of each party—said procedure providing more than adequate time to meet the Electoral College mandate. NOTE: Had this been the law in 2000, Al Gore would be our president, and the American economy would not be in meltdown!

7) Finally, absent the above safeguards, and until these safeguards are in place--Congress must mandate that PAPER BALLOTS, ONLY, can be used in our presidential elections. This is not a "partisan" issue, it is a "pro-democracy" issue. Most importantly, this will return the responsibility for our elections, and our vote counting, back into the hands of the individual voter, where it belongs, and out of the hands of "corporate control"--- *it is after all "our democracy", itself, that is at risk if we don't take these steps---and in that regard, is there*

any time or cost differential that is too great?

Jim Green

CHAPTER ELEVEN

FACEBOOK: TO CNN CAFFERTYFILE

Words are cheap! Romney brags that he can "get America working again"—that he can create 12 million jobs in his first year---So why is no one in the media asking Romney to explain—IN VERY SPECIFIC TERMS—exactly how he plans to do that? In truth, Romney's "method" is identical to Bush's method—which drove our economy into a ditch—and the American people need to know this! Jim Green, Democrat candidate for Congress, 2000

CHAPTER TWELVE

WHERE IS THE REPUBLICAN APOLOGY?

Futuristic fables such a "Rollerball" and "The Time Machine" propose scenarios for where us humans may be headed—

Too bad we don't have scenario with a rewind button, like our VCR, so we Americans could rewind and correct mistakes we made in the past—

For instance, let's say Justice Kennedy was ill that Saturday—and the U.S. Supreme Court didn't shut down the vote counting in Florida, and Al Gore— as all of the evidence shows to be correct—was elected president—

President Gore actually listened to the warnings from the CIA, and Massad [Israel's CIA] in August

2001—and by being on high alert—9-11 never happened—

No war on Iraq, or Afghanistan or on "terror"—No tens of thousands of lives lost--No $10 trillion hole for the American taxpayers to did themselves out----with $400 billion annually just to pay the interest on this debt, and trillions to mop up the mess this debt has caused—

And an economy so weakened by this deficit that our ability to dig out of this hole has been severely compromised—

But real tragedy is that absent a Republican apology [at an absolute minimum]—the Republican candidates for president, and in Congress are arrogant—like they pulled off the Brink's robbery and got away with it—

And incredulously that want to blame the Democrats, and America's progress over the past 70 years--for THEIR crimes!

But the most alarming—in the absence of an apology--the Republican agenda has not changed one iota!

It is still cut taxes for their wealthiest contributors, and add the short fall in revenue on to our deficit—they want to continue turning the American Dream, into America's Nightmare!

And absent an apology they intend to pick up right where Bush II left off!

CHAPTER THIRTEEN

To the editor/NY TIMES:

The Romney/Ryan faction are the grandchildren and children, respectively, of those Republicans who hated FDR, have fought Social Security from day one, and have been trying to decimate it for the past 77 years—it raises the question regarding this extremist faction of the Republican Party:

Do they hate old people, Do they hate the disabled—Do they hate everybody?

One thing is certain by the Ryan budget, alone— they want to cut Medicare and give the money to our billionaires!

Further, never has there been a more stark difference between their vision for America's future-

That is, the vision for America, between Republicans and Democrats, could not stand out in more bold relief in this election----and by putting Ryan on the ticket, Romney put the Republican agenda on a rocket ship straight into the 8th Century!

The Republicans want to roll back almost all of America's social progress of the past 200 years—and with women's rights as a special target—it makes you wonder if questioning their right to vote is just over the horizon?

As the bumper sticker so accurately defines [D] is for drive, and [R] is for reverse—so we have a very clear choice in this election—do we want to go forwards, or backwards?

My choice is [D]emocrat!

Jim Green, Democrat candidate for Congress, 2000 See also: "Why President Obama Lost The

2012 Election" on Amazon/Kindle [written to get our apathetic off their butts and vote for President Obama]

CHAPTER FOURTEEN

A response to the false stereotypes made about Democrats:

I really did like the letter from R L "Wake up Jim Green" —and I hope this letter will be printed as my response]—because she touches upon almost all of the stereotypes Republicans like to use in their talking points, about Democrats—and in not one case do they get it right—

Here goes: First, it is the Democrats who are concerned with what is in the best interest of the American people, and America—as opposed to the agenda of the national Republican Party, who are SOLELY interested in what is in the best economic interests of their richest contributors—PERIOD—

They have NO interest in the best economic well being of the "rank and file" who inexplicably vote Republican for a "national" office [the House, and above]—the agenda of the national Republican Party is about pandering to the GREED of their richest contributors—NOT working to create a better and stronger America—PERIOD!

Indeed, and as exhibit 1, the Republicans in Congress, today, are employing a political strategy to trash America—in the hopes that Obama will be blamed—and they will re-gain the White House—i.e., to use all extremes available—it is a "political" strategy that presumes the American people are really dumb—and it may backfire--

There is nuance in the specifics of my response— to quote: "Democrats have piddled away our tax dollars long enough pandering to political cronies and subsidizing 'free' give away programs to procure votes….".

There are several layers in this opinion—I'll take them one at a time, but not in sequence:

First we need to keep in mind that "projection" is a term used in Psychology—it is projecting, or ascribing OUR motives on to others—blaming them for OUR motives.

It was not the Democrats, but rather the Tea Party Republicans in Congress who played "politics" by taking America to the brink of bankruptcy—and losing our AAA credit rating in the world community!

These Republicans were running out the back door—TO AVOID PAYING BILLS THEY HAD CREATED! Raising the debt ceiling is to pay for bills we have already incurred—

It was the Republicans, alone, who doubled our deficit from $5 trillion to $10 trillion [the bills, above, they were trying to avoid paying]--during Bush II—they controlled all three branches of our government from 2001 to 2007—

And even when the American people regained their senses, and gave a majority of the House back to the Democrats, it was already too late—and Democrats also could not over-ride a presidential veto to stop this reckless and dangerous spending by the Republicans!

The [Democrats] "piddled away our tax dollars long enough" is interesting—

A popular pundit had as a stock question of Republican guests on his program: "Tell me what programs you would cut"? —and invariably they would get the same fumbleitis as Perry during the Republican debates—

For instance, should we do away with the Defense Department? By far, we spend more on our Defense/Intelligence community—than any other part of our federal budget—approaching $2 trillion annually--

Social Security Insurance has always been a "red herring"—which the Republicans derisively call an "entitlement" [is this one of the "give away" programs you are referring to Ms. L?]—

Social Security is an INSURNACE—it brings in more than it pays out—it does not add a dime to our deficit—and is very similar to our auto insurance—do you refer to your auto insurance as an "entitlement"?

Finally, Ms. L said that Democrats are motivated in creating programs, such as the GI Bill, Social Security Insurance, etc., to "procure votes"— WRONG—this is solely the province of the national Republican Party—

It is they who want you to distract the voters by having them talk about gay marriage, or gays in the military, etc., so they can tear down the EPA, and the Republicans have introduced 160 bills since January to undermine the protection of our environment—and for one reason: GREED!

What the "rank and file" who vote Republican don't seem to understand about our "Greed-Driven"—those have bought and paid for the Republicans in Congress—want your vote, alright—but meet them on the street and they would treat you like dirt on their shoes—and under their breath they call you jerks, and they think you are stupid—and given the facts---oh well, you figure it out….

Greed is like pornography, Ms. L—it has no socially redeeming value—

Jim Green

CHAPTER FIFTEEN

Editor/NYTimes:

Why have we gone nuts over paying taxes?

I never cease to be amazed how supportive and emotion-neutral we are in pooling our money for the benefit of all—when it comes to paying our auto insurance, or homeowner's insurance—

But go apoplectic and are emotion-charged when it comes to pooling our money for the benefit of all—when it comes to paying "taxes"—[Is it possible that paying taxes been soured by propaganda—by those who don't want to pay any—like the 1%]?

Also, tt seems to have something to do with "power"—[The rank and file Republicans appear to have contempt for Democrats, solely, because they win—like hating the opposing team if their team loses….rather than a concern for the betterment of America]…

We don't see people saying I am going to cancel my car insurance because claims are being paid to persons who are "black, or brown, or different, or just other humans"—but Republicans suddenly become xenophobic when it comes to paying taxes--

Also, some are OK so long as the taxes are going for Defense and prisons—but outraged when it goes out being our "brother's keeper"--

And we can't exclude propaganda-driven "greed" from the mix—

In short, we are all over the map when it comes to paying taxes—but are silent when it comes to paying our auto insurance—indeed, compulsory auto insurance is law [demanded by the public] in

almost every country in the world, including the
U.S.--

Jim Green, Democrat candidate for Congress,
2000

CHAPTER SIXTEEN

Editor/NYTimes:

The Republican invented term "American Exceptionalism"—is for losers....

I don't know about the rest of you but I find the new term used in right-wing propaganda— "American Exceptionalism"—and used quite frequently during the Republican debates—to be a particularly disturbing term—

For one, I have never met anyone yet who truly was "exceptional" –who found it necessary call themselves that—and conversely, it is spot-on correct in identifying persons who are suffering from low self-esteem—and prop themselves up by boasting—

Further, other countries looking at America, and coming to that conclusion—or not reaching this conclusion—are quite capable of reaching that conclusion on their own—without our finding it necessary to remind them—

And it has a particularly negative tone by suggesting to other countries—to borrow from a psychological term in "Games People Play"—"Mine's bigger than yours"—

Finally, the term is particularly disturbing because it suggests that as a world power—we are history—or at best, on our way out—and that calling ourselves "exceptional" is a last ditch, desperate grasp to remind other countries that we are the big cheese---

And the sooner this term is in the trash bin of history, the better—IMHO

Jim Green, Democrat candidate for Congress, 2000 [See also: My Letters To President Obama, on Amazon/Kindle]

CHAPTER SEVENTEEN

Editor/NYTimes:

I don't know about the rest of you but I am fed-up with all of the negative blather by the Republican candidates for president—against President Obama—

President Obama was handed a nightmare when he came into office—an economy in free-fall, and in the worst crash since the Great Depression.

What our expert economists [on the right and left] learned from the Great Depression is that the only prescription available is for our government to infuse cash, and plenty of it, into the economy to unfreeze an economy that had seized up—

It is the reason why the Bush administration infused almost a trillion dollars in TARP funds into our economy in 2008—and a like amount in "stimulus" money was appropriated by the Obama administration in early 2009—

And it is the exact same strategy that was used by the Reagan administration in 1987 when the stock market crashed on "Black Monday" resulting an almost 25% loss in one day—

During the Great Depression the FED concluded that to stop the Crash in 1929, that we should pull cash out of the economy—it was a terrible blunder—and accelerated our economic free-fall—turning what might have been a short-term recession, into the Great Depression it took us years to dig out of—

It is the reason every credible economist today urged the "stimulus" moneys President Obama used to prevent another Great Depression—

Politics being what they are, however, Republican strategists decided to appeal to our ignorant an uninformed by painting the "stimulus" used by President Obama—as wild spending by a "tax and spend" liberal—and this distorted lie persists by the Republican candidates for president to this day!

Also, it is unseemly and hypocritical for these candidates, as well as all of the Republicans in Congress, to now claim to be the champions of "deficit reduction"—WHEN IT IS REPUBLICAN POLICIES that handed President Obama a $10 trillion deficit when he came into office!

And to top it off the only solution offered by Republicans is to return to the same policies—THAT CAUSED OUR ECONOMIC MELTDOWN IN 2008—and the Republican One and Only job creations solution is based on the "Big Lie"!

It would be impossible to have 14 million Americans still unemployed if cutting taxes for the wealthy created jobs—BECAUSE THE BUSH TAX CUTS WERE EXTENDED!

So the next time Romney/Ryan demonize President Obama—remind them that they are Lying Hypocrites—and are stuffed between ears with rice pudding!

Jim Green, Democrat candidate for Congress, 2000   www.Inclusivism.org

CHAPTER EIGHTEEN

Editor/NY Times:

Where did these people come from, and why are they voting Republican?

The Republican Party has been mining our radical religious right, our racists, and our ignorant [per Ron Reagan], since the civil rights act of 1964—and they have doubled down since we now have a "black" president—

But when we superimpose an "economic representation" map over who the Republican Party represents—and the above faction—the overlap is zilch! Maybe one or two out of millions will show up in both maps!

Were a "representative" government folks. We hire people [our politicians] who "have our back"—to use a popular phrase—persons who are "in our corner"—and the agenda of the national Republican Party is to pander to the GREED of their wealthiest contributors-- PERIOD!

In short, they don't "represent" this faction—thus leaving the question—why would anyone in this faction who is in their right mind vote for a political party that doesn't "represent" them? [and please don't add "because they are not in their right mind"—the problem is far too serious for levity]….

But this is where it really gets interesting—with the Republicans Party's high dive into the abyss— and the two feeding off of each other—i.e., the Republican Party has become a magnet for candidates who want women barefoot, pregnant and in the kitchen—and with Paul Ryan and Congressman Akin, as Exhibit One!

Indeed, in adding Ryan to the ticket, Romney has strapped his agenda in this election to a rocket ship—straight into the 8th Century! And his energy plan for "drill baby drill" would send our melting ice cap into overdrive!

The bottom line is: Never has there been a more stark difference in the direction the respective parties want to take America—It's [D] for drive, and [R] for reverse—i.e., the Democrats want to move FORWARD into the 21st Century, while Romney wants to take us BACK to the Dark Ages!

Jim Green, Democrat candidate for Congress, 2000 [See also: "My Letters To President Obama" and "Why President Obama Lost The 2012 Election: A Wake-Up Call"—on Amazon/Kindle

CHAPTER NINETEEN

Editor/NYTimes:

Folks---We need to pull back the curtain and look at what is really behind the Republican agenda in this election:

First, we have tiny, tiny, tiny handful of Americans who are willing to chip in over a billion dollars to get Romney/Ryan elected—

And we need to drill down on who these folks are, and ask what do they want? For one, these are business people—they are not going to gamble that kind of cash unless they plan on getting a payoff for their gamble—

And their payoff, folks, is to have their taxes cut even further—so they can turn their billion dollars, into two billion—and not just via the tax cuts but also by hiding their cash in tax sheltered accounts in the Cayman Islands, etc., rather than investing in America, ad nauseam!

In short, folks—if this tiny, tiny, tiny handful [the 1%] is chipping in over a billion dollars to get Romney/Ryan elected--the last candidates us 99% should be voting for—is Romney/Ryan!

Jim Green, Democrat candidate for Congress, 2000

CHAPTER TWENTY

Editor/NYTimes:

Every informed voter needs to ask in this election:

Why on earth did America allow itself to be painted into the extreme, and radical position that if you are not an Adam Smith capitalist—you're a communist?

It is a position as hysterical as McCarthyism—and equally as dangerous—

There is little dispute, anywhere, that America turned down this dark alley when the U.S. Supreme Court gave corporations a blank check to buy our elections!

And "Super Pacs" started cropping up all over the place, and the Norquist Pledge—threatening persons running for Congress—"raise taxes, and we will spend millions to defeat you"—

AND NO accountability to disclose the source of their funds!

We got our first taste of this corrupt buying of our elections in 2010—when the House was bought and paid for with this "blood money" ["money gotten ruthlessly at the expense of others' suffering"]—and in this case the victims are the American people!

For instance, this new crop of radicals in the House have introduced 160 bills [and counting] since January 2011—to destroy our environmental protection laws—so that corporations can drill the Rocky Mountains down to an ant hill!!

And they have made crystal clear that they intend to use the American people as a battering ram—

under the devious political agenda to undermine
President Obama—

It as contemptible, as well as hypocritical, by
claiming to now be the champion of deficit
reduction—when it Republican policy THAT
CAUSED THE DEFICIT!

Jim Green, Democrat candidate for Congress,
2000

CHAPTER TWENTY-ONE

Editor/NYTimes:

Mitch McConnell said after the debt ceiling talks at the White House on July 10, 2011—that it is "baffling that the president and his party continue to insist on massive tax hikes in the middle of a jobs crisis."

Is there anyone with half a brain in America who cannot see that this statement is a phony as three-dollar bill?

First, the "massive" he is talking about is Exxon giving up the $5 billion in subsidies they got from us, the American people—while sticking it to us at the pump—and recording the highest profits in American history—for starters!

But here is the real con job in that statement—the "Big Lie" being perpetrated on the American people by the Republicans in Congress is that tax cuts for the wealthy will magically translate into jobs!

Well hey, Senator McConnell the Bush tax cuts were extended so why do we have 14 million Americans still unemployed—where are all those jobs that you promised us if we continued the Bush tax cuts last December?

And why were 10 times more private sector jobs created when Clinton was president—and the tax rates on the most wealthy was raised from 35% to 39%--than at any time during the entire Bush II presidency?

McConnell said that his single objective from the day President Obama was elected—was to prevent his re-election in the 2012 election [consummate proof that McConnell had no interest in working on behalf of the American people]—but since President Obama had no record which would justify this judgment by McConnell—is there any explanation other than McConnell is a racist pig—and that he was speaking to his like kind…..?

So why don't we tell the truth in America? And where is our media in calling McConnell out on this racist statement?

Jim Green, Democrat candidate for Congress, 2000

CHAPTER TWENTY-TWO

Editor/NY Times:

Doesn't it strike anyone as odd that Paul Ryan
rails, daily, over deficits under President Obama—
indeed, holding himself out, now, as a champion
of deficit reduction—WHEN he voted to drive up
our deficit by over $7 trillion, while in Congress,
under Bush II!

Actually, "odd" may be too kind—maybe
"disingenuous" [which is the polite way to say
someone is a lying SOB]—"Aw shucks", Ryan is a
lying hypocrite—it is the only honest description
that fits!

And to add insult to injury, Ryan now wants to
decimate [i.e., destroy] Medicare—[read Ryan's
Budget]--so he can give the money saved to the
Republican's wealthiest contributors—their payoff
for getting him elected! What a guy!

We won't even go to his Draconian approach regarding "women's rights", [including being anti-choice]—and evident by his co-sponsoring legislation with Akin, Ad Nauseam!

And he is doing all of this while claiming to be a "Christian" [actually Catholic]—seems he has forgotten that if one is not following the teachings of Christ, one is NOT a Christian! Which the "Nuns On A Bus" have been quick to remind him!

And if the reader does not know that the sole agenda of the National Republican Party, the same as Ryan, is to make the rich, richer—and them poorer—they are not paying attention!

But getting back to the deficit, please consider this metaphor: If one of our children spills a glass of milk—we wipe it up with some paper towels—but if they spill a whole gallon—we grab a mop and a bucket and everything else at hand to clean up the mess—

And, President Obama was handed a mega-spill to clean up—from day one—as a direct result of the mess caused by Ryan, and the rest of the Republicans over the past 8 years!

In short, it cost us—the American taxpayers $5 trillion just to clean up the $10 trillion mess left by the Republicans, i.e., it was this "mop and bucket" President Obama had to use to prevent another Great Depression!

Finally, you would think Romney and company would, first, profusely apologize to the American people for the mess they left—and then promise never to pull this gimmick on the American people again—
But they have the gall to tell us they are going to double-down—i.e., pick up right where Bush II left off!

Do they think we are stupid? Don't answer that....

Jim Green, Democrat candidate for Congress, 2000 [See also: "My Letters To President Obama", and "Why President Obama Lost The 2012 Election: A wake-up call", on Amazon/Kindle

CHAPTER TWENTY-THREE

Editor/NYTimes:

What we have learned from the Republican primaries—is that a tiny, tiny handful of Americans have crowded the Republican Party into a such a reactionary and radical corner that it has become like a Black Hole in space—so impacted by extremism that light can barely escape—

And we know this by what they are talking about as "issues"—and by how few Americans are showing up to vote—

For instance, in Maine ALL of the Republican candidates received only one-half of one percent of those eligible to vote—99.5 % were absentee—as one pundit observed, the "R" in Republican has come to mean "Racists and Radicals", i.e., they are the only ones who are showing up to vote—

Regarding issues—women are not to use contraceptives—and if they get pregnant [even if via a rape] they cannot terminate the pregnancy—in short they want to put "Rosie the Riveter" back in the kitchen—barefoot and pregnant—can ending her right to vote be far behind?

Also, another pundit observed--98% of women use contraceptives, and the other 2% are lying—even disregarding that it is patently irresponsible given our teen pregnancy, and married or unmarried, to venture into parenthood in the reckless method this Republican policy advocates!

Also, the lack of civility in our current political discourse has become so coarsened as to be alarming.

To make the distinction, war hero and former Senator Bob Dole said it best when he said President Clinton is "My opponent, not my enemy"—but much of the rhetoric today is an appeal to persons who want to de-humanize President Obama.

In short, being critical of bad policy, as above, is essential to our getting good government—de-humanizing a person, or group, is the tactic used to carry out the Holocaust—

The truth is, President Obama was handed a nightmare, and he deserves a solid "A" for what he got right—i.e., the vitriolic rhetoric is baseless, devoid of logic or the facts—and has cheapened even "political" prattle--

And it is unthinkable that we would hand America back to the spineless Republicans—who have placed "politics" [appealing to these nuts cases]—over what is in the best interests of America!

In short, we have a tiny handful of racists and radicals in the Republican Party drowning out any semblance of sanity and civility in our political discourse, today—and a 24-7 news cycle handing them the mic--so they can sell soap—i.e., will "Greed and Ignorance" finally do us in?

Jim Green, Democrat candidate for Congress, 2000 www.Inclusivism.org

CHAPTER TWENTY–FOUR

Editor/NYTimes:

A number of our new congresspersons are threatening to dismantle the healthcare reforms by the Democrats [which actually didn't go far enough]—but we need to ask, why on earth would they even consider doing this?

The only persons complaining about the reforms made by Democrats to our healthcare system—are persons who do not understand the healthcare system we have now [and this can also be said about many of the reforms over the past 2 years]—

For instance, America is the only country in the world that permits their health insurance companies to make a "profit" off of people getting healthcare—

After all, our health insurance companies don't even so much as put a Band-Aid on a patient— they are simply a pass-through agent—we pool our money to brace against the high costs of healthcare, if we need it [as with all other insurance] and they pay out our claims--[and as a footnote, a metaphor we should adopt in paying taxes—where we pool our money for our individual protection, and for the common good]--

As it has turned out our health insurance companies have turned this "pass through" thing they do—not just into a way to make a little money in the process—but rather into a Texas-sized bonanza---a gold mine at the expense of our health--this is not a big business—it is a big, big, big business—with obscene salaries for their CEO's, etc—

For instance, our health insurance companies have six lobbyists for each of the 435 Members of Congress, and 100 members of the Senate—all with six figure salaries--as I write—and all are there for only one reason—to protect the pot of gold the health insurance companies are making off of the American people!

But the real wake-up call—for those who do not understand the reforms made by the Democrats—every dime of those salaries to lobbyists came from money they sent in in premiums—money intended for the healthcare of Americans, not to enrich the health insurance companies!

This also explains why we are 37th in the world in the quality of healthcare in America, according to the World Health Organization—and we have a mortality rate along side some Third World countries!

In summing up—and for clarity---sell a car, make a buck—absolutely, that is the America way—but making a "profit" off of people's health should be a criminal offense—

Jim Green, Democrat candidate for Congress, 2000 www.Inclusivism.org

CHAPTER TWENTY–FIVE

I saved the best for last [I couldn't resist including this]…. This chapter is dedicated to our Teavangelicals, and assorted nuts courted by the Republican Party—and which are, at best, strange bedfellows—because it is impossible to be Christian—and vote for anything the Republicans stand for:

A MESSAGE FROM GOD

MANY CENTURIES AGO, a man of the cloth, we don't know his name, and in a flash of insight (perhaps induced by peyote) told his flock that "sex is a sin". And lo and behold he learned that by taking a very natural and healthy part of our life and turning it into something that was "dirty and nasty", that he could imprison his flock, and fill his coffers, and hallelujah it was a great day for the Lord!

Quickly, his miracle spread to other churches in his village, and then to the next village, and then the next county and then state and then it spread to all the churches in the ancient world, and all of their flocks cowed in fear and shame and became imprisoned, and their coffers over-floweth. Hallelujah, it was a great day for the Lord!

And to keep the myth alive they started inventing stories, half-baked stories, that made no sense to anyone who is rational, such as "Mary was a virgin"—well, she just had to be a virgin because she would never partake in anything that was dirty and nasty, like sex (if you're doing it right), and this was necessary to make "sex is a sin" make sense...so they invented a Mary that was "sinless"-- you get the picture. And it is apparent that God had to make sex very pleasurable just to overcome all the bullshit. And their coffers over-floweth. Hallelujah, it was a great day for the Lord!

No one seemed to be bothered that when we play tricks on the human mind by taking something that is very natural and healthy, such as sex, and make it dirty and nasty that all kinds of bad things happen to the human mind.

Such as most pedophiles, and most serial killers, and voting Republican, and unwarranted suicides, and most mental illness, and unwanted pregnancies. (Teens not wanting to have sex is the perversion, not the other way around, and by replacing sex education and condoms, with unrealistic "abstinence", and by using blather about "low self-esteem" to shame them into not "sinning"--We have a teen pregnancy in the U.S. twice that of England and Canada!).

But none of this mattered, because their coffers over-floweth, and Hallelujah, it is a great day for the Lord!

There is a cure--------Tell these right-wing loonies to shove it....

GOD

ABOUT THE AUTHOR: I was employed in our Criminal Justice System for a cumulative 20 years as a probation officer, with 5 of those years as a chief probation officer. I authored the concept of "Shock Incarceration" which became law in Kansas in 1970, and then was adopted in numerous jurisdictions in the U.S. and also spread to Europe—it is currently identified in the U.S. as "Boot Camp" [as the means to "shock" the young offender—and a total distortion of my original intent—like many ideas, once released, they take on a life of their own]. I was the Democrat candidate for Congress, District 21, TX, 2000. I would most define myself as a Social Ecologist-- [albeit my degree is in Psychology]. My web page is www.Inclusivism.org —which has been on the internet since 1996.

Other books by the author on Amazon/Kindle:

MY LETTERS TO PRESIDENT OBAMA, LETTERS ON
STEROIDS, THE HARVARD BOYS CLUB [my first],
WHY PRESIDENT OBAMA LOST THE 2012
ELECTION: A Wake-Up Call [for our amnesic],
and THE FIRST TIME I HAD SEX [a response to our
oppressive radical religious right]

www.ingramcontent.com/pod-product-compliance
Lightning Source LLC
Chambersburg PA
CBHW072329290526
45794CB00002B/800